NON-DUAL TEACHINGS OF THE BIBLE

To Karla
with gratitude
for your insightful
help with this book
Galen Sharp

GALEN SHARP

ISBN: 0994377932
ISBN-13: 978-0-9943779-3-7

Author's photo by Glenn Cuerden

Non-Dual Teachings Of The Bible/ by
Galen Sharp

Portions of this book have appeared in other writings by Galen Sharp

Printed in the United States of America

River of Life Publications
www.riveroflifepublications.com

What difference can non-duality make in our understanding of the Bible?
It appears to hold the key to a deeper understanding of "Walking in the Spirit" as well as open a new perspective on the profound mystery of "Oneness with God."

To Bobbie, my wife

ACKNOWLEDGMENTS

To Karla Rae Harper for her insightful suggestions, Bible knowledge, excellent advice and encouragement.

To Natasha and David Rivers, my publishers for their hard work, encouragement and commitment to publishing this book.

CONTENTS

Chapter 1: When We Were Very Young

"...The Kingdom of God has arrived."
– Mark 1:15

Remember how it used to be when you were very young, the freedom of just being? You lived in the present effortlessly and spontaneously. Each day was faced as a joyous adventure, not reluctantly, as something to be endured.

Once in a while we half-remember this freedom with deep nostalgia, wondering what ever happened to that specialness, that effortless joy and the open wonder we once knew long ago. Where did it go? The harder we try to recapture it, the more elusive it seems to be.

The best of the "Good News" is that it is actually *still here and now.* This way of effortless living never went away. It is still here and always has been. It has instead become veiled and distorted by illusion, an illusion that arises because of the way our thought mechanism works and because we have accepted what others have told us we were and what the world was. They too live in their own version of that same illusion, and have unwittingly passed the deceptive virus on to us.

We assume that it is just the way life is. As we get older, we take on responsibilities, life gets more difficult, and that's just the way it is. We grew up. But alas, we didn't grow up we actually grew down. This is because we let others define our identity, tell us who we were. And we acquired the same world model that they lived in. But remember this: when we were young and living this life of freedom we were also learning the language, how to walk and many other new things. Those are great responsibilities and yet it did not affect that joyous sense of freedom. Of course we didn't recognize it then, but we were actually living in what the Bible calls the Kingdom of Heaven. As, witness, "Truly, I say unto you, and unless you turn and become like children you will never enter the Kingdom of Heaven." [Matthew 18:3 RSV[1]] "But Jesus called unto him, and said, suffer little children to come unto me, and forbid them not: for of such is the Kingdom of God." [Luke 18:16] Thus, the Kingdom of God is not some place you go *after* you die! It is available here and now!

---

1 Scripture quotes are from the King James Version unless otherwise noted.

"The Kingdom of God is among you, but you recognize it not." [Luke 17:21] *So why don't we recognize it then?* It is because we are living from a *dualistic* point of view and that blinds us and keeps us from recognizing the Kingdom. We'll look at that in much more detail shortly.

This book isn't as much about gaining something as it is about losing something. And that is your false illusions that hide what is already within you. For you already have this spiritual insight within you. But it is hidden by dualistic assumptions. It is just a matter of seeing through the illusions that we have acquired in our belief system. Once you see through an illusion it dissolves on its own to reveal the truth it is hiding.

FROM CURIOSITY TO DESPERATION

This author, like many others, had been raised a nominal Christian. Also, like many others, I thought Christianity was just about being a good person and never really understood what the crucifixion was all about. I knew only that if I was a Christian I would go to heaven when I died.

So, being a young Christian, I had tried to be a good person. Usually I could do fairly well at it, but soon found I couldn't always be good and eventually lost interest. It was just too hard.

Then, years later, when I discovered that my self image, "me," was not what I really was and, was just an illusion (more on that later) I also wondered briefly what my "real self" was. But I didn't follow up on that then. Eventually though, after several months of being thrilled about not having to live up to a false self image, I began to really search for what I actually was. I went from curiosity gradually to desperation. What was I really? Where was my real self? I then turned to the Bible where I came onto a verse in John, verse 1:9. "That was the true light which lighteth every man that cometh into the world." However, I still didn't really understand how that would help me, though it was a big clue. But this did lead me to discover there was more to Christianity than I had realized. I assumed all Christians understood that the self was an illusion. I became interested in Christianity because I thought I could find out what I was.

To give the reader a better idea of what I went through in the search for an authentic self here are some of the highlights.

THE SEARCH FOR A SELF

When I first became interested in Christianity I was filled with joy and love and looked forward to a new life. But after a while the "newness" wore off and I began to find it increasingly difficult to live the Christian life that I sincerely wanted to live. It was the same old story again! I would pray and ask God for help, but the harder I tried the more difficult it became. Old habits began to pull me back. I went here and there and listened to various preachers and Bible teachers. But as good as they sounded, still nothing helped. Somehow it still wasn't working for me and whenever I would ask someone about Christ being our real self they didn't know what I was talking about.

For the most part I could look good on the outside, but in my heart I knew I wasn't living up to the ideals I sought. What was I to do? I had thought all I needed was to know what to do and then I could do it and Christ would help me. But I found that didn't work.

Then one day while reading the Bible I found another important clue. I was reading Romans and discovered in Chapter 7 that the apostle Paul had exactly the same problem as I. "For that which I do I allow not: for what I would, that I do not; but what I hate, that do I." [Romans 7:15] In other words he does what he knows he shouldn't do and isn't able to do what he should do. Boy, I sure could identify with that.

Excited, I was following right along until I got to the end of Chapter 7, "O wretched man that I am! Who shall deliver me from *this body of death*? I thank God through Jesus Christ our Lord. So then with the mind I serve the Law of God; but with the flesh the law of sin." [Romans 7:24, 25] Then Romans 8 starts with, "There is therefore now no condemnation to them which are *in Christ Jesus, who walk not after the flesh, but after the spirit.*[2] For the law of the spirit of life in Christ Jesus hath made me *free* from the law of sin and death. For that which the law could not do, in that it was weak through the flesh, God sending his own Son in the likeness of sinful flesh, and for sin, condemned sin in the flesh: that the righteousness of the law might be fulfilled in us, who walk not after the flesh, but after the Spirit." [Romans 8:1-4]

I didn't understand. First, what is "this body of death" (in Romans 7:14) and second, how does one "walk after the Spirit?" It seemed to skip a whole chapter in that gap between Romans 7 and Romans 8.

I know now that walking after the Spirit is effortless when you understand it from the non-dual perspective! Walking after the Spirit isn't supposed to be difficult and hard, but spontaneous

---

2 More commonly known as "walking in the Spirit." But we will use the Biblical phrase here.

and natural, easy, free and joyous. "For my yoke is easy and my burden is light." [Matthew 11:30] It is not a matter of trying to second guess God, and then doing it or constantly asking yourself, is that from God or me?

In the meantime, I had already achieved some of my most important goals in life. I was the art director for a national advertising agency and was earning more than many my age. I had a beautiful, loving wife and two wonderful children. But yet I still didn't feel fulfilled. I was working nearly 80 hours a week and wasn't able to spend much time with my family.

No matter what I achieved, it didn't seem to make much difference except briefly and I always ended up feeling unhappy and unfulfilled again. The mind kept telling me, once I get this, I'll be happy. Then when I got it, the mind always came up with yet another thing I needed in order to be happy. And on and on it went.

The mind lies to us.

Then one day I began to wonder just what it would really take to make me feel fulfilled and happy. So I tried to imagine what level of achievement would it take to actually make me happy and fulfilled.

No matter what I could imagine I could always find insecurities and situations that would lead to problems and unhappiness. Even if I were ruler of the world, I would still have problems and most probably even worse ones! Yes, things would always be going wrong and, on top of that, I still couldn't live up to my own ideals.

Then, I came upon the intuitive realization that if I can't be happy in the here and now, I won't be happy in the future no matter what I achieve.

With that realization I went into a deep depression that lasted longer than I care to say. Eventually, all this brought me to again start wondering *what* I really was. What am I that I can't just be happy in the present and do what I should and not do what I shouldn't? That might possibly give me a clue to my unhappiness.

However I had previously searched within myself for a self, and had realized that I could find only thoughts and ideas about what I was, but no real "self." I could only find the bare sense of "I am." Yet I could find no self or an actual "me." However I still remembered John 1:9 "That was the true light which lighteth every man that cometh into the world." What could it really mean? Could this somehow be my "real" self? After all, the word "light" is often used to mean "consciousness," as in "the light of consciousness."

To give the reader a sense of where I was let's try this experiment now. I will call such spiritual research an “Exercise.” Their purpose is to bypass the dualistic, rational mind and open the spiritual, non-dual, nonlinear sense.

You must actually DO each Exercise and not just imagine doing it no matter how simple they might appear. They are to open your spiritual eyes and unless you actually do them they won’t have the same effect. If you are serious about understanding this you will do them.

EXERCISE # 1
THE I CHART

Make a chart of who you are. Start with your name at the top and labels down the left. Then write down the answers to these questions.

Name?
Where do I live?
Where was I born?
What is my gender?
What do I look like physically?
What are my hobbies?
Am I married?
Do I have children?
What are my treasures?
What are my strengths?
What are my weaknesses?
What are my most important accomplishments?
What is my best memory?
What is my worst memory?
What ethnic group do I belong to?
What is my religion?

This is briefly who you think you are.

Now, ask yourself these questions: (Don't rush them. Pause for a while with each one and really focus on it. Try to look deeper than your first assumption.)

1. Is this really me?

2. Or is this simply a list of labels, ideas, memories, concepts?

3. If I had no labels would I still exist?

4. Who or what would I be then?

5. Does this thought upset me?

6. Instead of focusing on your label self, why not speculate upon what your "True Self" could be?

If and when we do actually look for what we are, all we can find are concepts and ideas. Try this yourself right now. Most people never think to look for a self. They just assume they are one. Look for an actual self that isn't just a thought or a feeling.

What did you find?

You see, we must go deeper than concepts, ideas and feelings to try to find the actual source of it all.

When I realized that my "self" was just an idea, a shifting, unstable concept, my self image, I had felt incredibly liberated! I realized I had been a slave all my life to a mere concept, trying to satisfy it, protect it and make it look good. I felt the burden of this self fall away and I was free! At the time, I didn't know yet what I was, but I still felt amazingly liberated. The self wasn't real and I no longer had to take care of its relentless demands. Society could no longer use it to manipulate me.

My concept of self was constantly changing and was never stable. It was affected by moods and circumstances. You are good when things go right, but not good when things don't go well. It is ever shifting like the sands of the desert.

Our belief system

One of the reasons I was having difficulty understanding these things is what is called our "belief system." A set of mutually supportive beliefs classified as, religious, philosophical, ideological or a combination of these.

This is because we have incorporated our belief system into our self concept. It has become a part of who we think we are. And we are questioning this self concept.

Because of this way the mind works, many things that are contrary to our belief system are automatically discounted by the mind at the subconscious level and not even seen at all and we don't even realize we are rejecting them. Anything that challenges our belief system is seen as a challenge to our self, and it is automatically resisted. That's why you may need to read through this book several times because your belief system and worldview will blind you to some of the most important parts of it. And you won't even know it is happening. Intelligence and education do not make one immune to this.

OUR WORLDVIEW

A large part of our belief system is built upon our world model or worldview, which is our particular conception of the world or the way we view reality. Thus, things contrary to our worldview are also resisted, either consciously or unconsciously.

Our worldview is another one of the things we will examine. When we begin to scrutinize it in the here and now we will discover some surprising things that will be upsetting to our present worldview and to our present belief system. But don't be afraid to question them because they are a big reason for our bondage and suffering.

We began to form the basics of our worldview including our belief system when we were very young. Therefore, for the largest part, we have learned it from *other people.*

The problem with that is it has some serious flaws, especially at the most important part, the basic foundation, built when we were very young when we easily misunderstood things. And the foundation determines how the whole structure will grow. But, since we feel that it is a part of our self, our subconscious mind and emotions strongly resist anything that questions it as if it were questioning our self. That frightens and confuses us. Our first instinct is to just flat out reject it and turn away from it. "It's not the way I learned it," we say to ourselves. We feel we don't need to have our most cherished opinions questioned. But that would be a mistake.

Unfortunately, some of our Christian assumptions are influenced by our learned worldview and are, of course, mixed in with our belief system. At the same time it is why we can't or don't understand many verses in the Bible. This is why, in the beginning, some of the things we will be examining may be unsettling. But, if we are brave and adventurous, when we have finally broken through, our faith and understanding will be a great deal simpler, clearer and absolutely unshakable.

Also, in the back of our mind, is always that secret voice of doubt that we may not have it all "right," that we may be mistaken or deceived in some aspect of our faith. This makes us afraid to closely examine some of our long-held assumptions about what we call reality. We may feel a great need to be "one of the right ones" and be sure of our salvation, so we are not receptive to close reflection about our assumptions. At the same time we secretly feel insecure about the "rightness" of some of our assumptions, and don't want to rock the boat.

THE TRUTH SHALL MAKE YOU FREE

However by fearlessly facing and examining the foundation of our worldview we will be able to get to the bottom of it all and, maybe for the first time, see through all the confusion, illusion and doubt to the unshakeable, rock-solid insight that literally opens us to another, higher dimension of living... the Kingdom of Heaven.

It is like the surf at the beach. Near the shore we are buffeted by waves and rough waters. This can cause confusion and fears. But if we continue on, the water smooth's out and soon becomes calm.

A NEW WORLDVIEW

All one can ever prove empirically is that perceptions are spontaneously appearing in consciousness. We can't prove that there is a three dimensional world "out there." And any scientific tools we might use to prove a three dimensional world are also manifested phenomenally by our perceptions.

Proof of this can be seen by examining how dreams are manifested in our sleep. In the dream a three dimensional world appears, though it actually takes up no space in our bedroom. But in the dream is all the space we need. Most important, we seem also to be in a three dimensional, material world just as we are when awake. Nevertheless that world comes and goes with the dream. However, when in the dream we would swear that the dream world is made up of "things-in-themselves." That is many individual "things." Yet, after waking, upon reflection, we realize that all the seemingly separate things, as well as the other people, are comprised of only percepts. All the things and people in the dream had no actual material substance. Science will tell us the "real" world is the same. "Matter is derived from consciousness, not consciousness from matter." – Sir James Jeans, noted British scientist. And the Bible tells us the same thing. "Through faith we understand that the worlds were framed by the word of God, so that things which are seen were not made of things which do appear." [Hebrews 11.3]

NON-DUALITY TO THE RESCUE

This is where our understanding of "reality" and our worldview clashes with both science and the Bible. Our inherited worldview seems to work pretty well, but we are unaware of what it has cost us in terms of our own peace, liberty and joy. Not to mention our relationship with God.

This is where non-duality comes to the rescue, as we shall discover. Because of our dualistic way of understanding, what we perceive takes on the character of things-in-themselves, that is a world of separate, pre-existing things and people apart from other things and people. Therefore, when we think of God and our self we can only, logically, see this as two separate entities. God seems to be a separate entity and I am another separate entity. This is something we probably have never thought about. This is why it is so difficult to comprehend being "hidden with Christ in God." While that suggests to us not one, not even two, but actually three entities – our self, Jesus, and God. However, we have forgotten we are speaking of Spirit here. Not three separate spirits. For, as we see in [Genesis 2:7 AB] "...God...breathed into his nostrils the breath or Spirit of life, and man became a living soul." So Adam's life was Gods life, God's Spirit. Jesus, as God's son is also of the same Spirit. Thus, we have *one* Spirit instead of three separate ones. Yet, not even one because Spirit is not a "thing" or even a substance. It is sentient life. It can only be visualized phenomenally as being prior to or "upstream" of manifestation. So it is not even one!

Imagine a large TV screen with many picture-in-picture scenes. Imagine that our life is one of them. We don't notice the colorless, clear, still screen, but only the images projected on it. Their only existence is on the screen. In a similar way the clear light of consciousness "here" is not noticed while we are occupied with the images appearing in it. In the same way, we see the forms and never notice the clear light of consciousness in which they appear. That is because it has no shape or form or color. Yet the real existence of the images is in consciousness.

In trying to understand the non-dual aspect we can visualize it as pertaining to *actions* of the senses rather than things-in-themselves. (Those senses are seeing, hearing, tasting, touching smelling and thinking.) In other words, two dualistic things-in-themselves are expressed in one sensorial action – seeing. For instance the sense of seeing embodies the dualistic interdependent pair – the object seen and the seer of the object. Notice that, in a dream the actual object "seen" and the subject "seer" are simply perceptions of seeing appearing as the dualism "seer and seen." but do not exist in the dream as actual, "real" objects. There is only the non-dual action of *seeing* wherein the seer and seen are dualistically interpreted as two objects. But as we know the objects (seer and seen) did not actually exist as things-in-themselves in the dream. They are simply perceptions arising in consciousness and interpreted as *things* because of our dualistic worldview. Therefore "seeing" infers an object as "seer" and an object "seen." However, neither object exists as an object-in-itself, only the perceptions of "seeing" are happening.

Dare I suggest that this real, waking world is manifested the same way! Throughout history, wise men, sages, holy men and now scientists have been trying to tell us it is. "Things that are seen were not made of things which do appear." [Hebrews 11:3]

Now don't jump to the conclusion that "it's all in my head" for this includes the perceptions of our head and body also. This may seem complicated and abstruse reading it here for the first time, but don't give up! Once recognized, it is very simple.

If that doesn't turn our worldview upside down and inside out then I don't know what will. See Acts 17:6. Yet we will find that when we understand this, the Bible will open to a deeper, more profound level and we will see it much more clearly. Continue on to see why this is so important. It is the key to understanding our oneness with God.

CHAPTER 2: ADAM AND EVE – PARADISE LOST

"Closer is He than breathing, nearer than hands and feet."
– Tennyson

To find out why we can't find a real self, but only the illusion of one, let's go back and visit Adam and Eve in the Garden of Eden. We will also explore why we can only interpret or make sense of the terms "good" and "evil" if we believe we are an individual, objective self.

"Then the Lord God formed man from the dust of the ground, and breathed into his nostrils the breath of life or Spirit; and man became a living soul." [Genesis 2:7AB] The "breath of life" is sentient awareness. The sense of "I am." God's own Spirit.

"And the Lord God commanded the man (Adam) saying, Of every tree of the garden thou mayest freely eat; But of the tree of the knowledge of good and evil, thou shalt not eat of it; for in the day thou shalt eatest thereof thou shalt surely die." [Genesis 2: 16, 17] Notice that God didn't call it "the tree of knowledge," as many believe, but the tree of the knowledge of *good and evil.*" That's important as you will soon find out.

"And the serpent said unto the woman, Ye shall not surely die; For God doth know that in the day ye eat thereof, then your eyes shall be opened, and ye shall be as God, *knowing good and evil.* And when the woman saw that the tree was good for food, and that it was pleasant to the eyes, and a tree to be desired to make one wise, she took of the fruit thereof, and did eat, and gave also to her husband with her; and he did eat. And the eyes of the both of them were opened, *and they knew that they were naked*, and they sewed fig leaves together, and made themselves aprons." [Genesis 3: 4-7]

"And he (Adam) said, I heard thy voice in the garden and I was afraid because I was naked; and I hid myself. And He (God) said, Who told thee that thou wast naked? (Here Adam has identified with his body as his self.) Hast thou eaten of the tree, whereof I commanded thee that thou shouldst not eat? And unto Adam He said, because thou hast harkened unto the voice of thy wife, and hast eaten of the tree. Which I commanded thee, saying Thou shalt not eat of it: cursed is the ground for thy sake*; in sorrow shalt thou eat of it all the days of thy life.*" [Genesis 3:10, 11, 17]

How then did they die? [re: Genesis 2:17]

While their bodies were not dead but still alive, how they knew themselves and the world had changed dramatically and they actually fell down into a lower dimension, a dimension of dead, empty concepts. So this "body of death" is the conceptual self, "me." To themselves, they were no more one with God, but were each a separate conceptual entity which included body and mind. This is proven by the fact that they hid themselves from God and "knew" they were naked. So they were definitely identifying with their bodies. The moment they thought of (conceptualized) themselves as their body, they saw themselves as a separate, objective entity apart from God and no longer one with God and all phenomenality. And that is the way we have known ourselves ever since. We conceptualize our body (along with the mind) as our selves. This is what psychologists call "self awareness" and believe it is a good thing.

Another proof is that one can have no concept of good and evil unless one objectifies and identifies with one's body, that is, conceptualizes themselves as a separate "object" (body) in a world of other things. Think about this...

Then good and bad things can happen to this imagined object, "me," this body/mind. If you didn't think you were a separate body/mind, good and evil would be irrelevant. You see, before that, they were naturally one with God and the world. Everything was spontaneously happening as it should.

And what exactly happened to cause that fall? It is because their minds began to operate in a different way, dualistically, so that they could make concepts from the perceptions and conceptualize. (That is make a "thought label" for the apparent things-in-themselves.) Then they made a concept of what they were as an individual body/mind, a separate, volitional "me." And that gave meaning to the terms "good" and "evil." That is how being able to conceptualize made them "wise." Words are just conceptual labels representing a group of perceptions.

The moment one begins to think of oneself as an individual entity or identity, one is seemingly separate from everyone and everything else in the world, *including God!*

While this concept of a separate self is untrue, it has the same effect in the mind as though it were true. Everything that happens or could happen is immediately judged in the mind as to how it will affect this individual body/mind concept, "me." This creates desires and fears for the conceptual self in the belief system and that, in turn, strongly influences all subsequent actions and thoughts.

It also makes one "self centered" whether we want that or not.

This, friends, is the "Fall of Man." And the death God warned about is losing our identity with God and becoming, *in the mind,* nothing more than the empty, dead objective concept, "me." And now since the Tree of Life is barred from them, the body also will physically die in the future. We are a seemingly separate "me" in our thoughts and belief. That separate conceptual "me" can never know true oneness with God. That is conceptually and logically impossible. By its very definition it is a separate, individual being. This is the "body of death" that the apostle Paul referred to in Romans 7:24. Reference: "Let the dead bury their dead." [Luke 9:60]

That's the knowledge of "good and evil" or good and bad. This is enabled and caused by the new ability for dualistic thought. Dualistic thought is the way we form concepts like "self" and "other." The concept "self" gets its meaning by being the opposite of "other." And "other" gets its meaning by being the opposite of "self." They are mutually exclusive and yet interdependent. They are simply and only thoughts, nothing real or substantial in themselves. They *represent* just a group of *perceptions in awareness.* Other simple dualistic concepts are "up" and "down," "far" and "near" as well as the infamous "good" and "evil." In fact all conceptual thought works this way, dualistically by forming concepts by comparison with other concepts. It is a little like the mythical island Lewis Carroll told about where the inhabitants made a precarious living by taking in each other's washing.

God placed two cherubim with flaming swords (representing dualism?) to guard Eden and the tree of life. See Genesis 3:24. As long as we are living in dualistic concepts, we can't recognize the Kingdom of Heaven. That's why most Bible scholars believe the Kingdom has not yet arrived. They not only refuse to enter the Kingdom themselves, but they block the way for others. "...for ye shut up the Kingdom of Heaven against men: for ye neither go in yourselves, neither suffer them that are entering to go in." [Matthew 23:13]

However, the dualistic thought process *has* "made us wise" and enabled us to build the technical world we have today, such as it is. And it has put us higher than the animals in intellect. Yet we don't even suspect that this "great gift" of conceptual thought has come at a horrific cost. We exist in a "living death" by identifying ourselves with the empty, dead, concept "me," along with the body.

Here we are in this wonderful, technically advanced, futuristic world and yet we are alone, depressed and desperate, separate from God, man, and nature. We may have advanced technically, but we haven't advanced as sentient beings. Instead we are adversaries with each other and all of nature.

A NEW HOPE

When we become a Christian, we believe we have found an end to our suffering with the promise that this will be the end of our alienation from God and we have the answer to living happily ever after.

And it actually seems to work in the beginning and we are happy and fulfilled and are looking forward to a wonderful adventure. But then, slowly at first, we begin to lose our initial momentum and begin to slip back into our old feelings and habits. Most of us are able to hide this at first, even from ourselves. We want to revive our initial faith and hope and make good as a Christian.

But, if we are honest with ourselves, it is not really happening. We rev up our emotions and seek uplifting experiences to satisfy ourselves that we are on the right course. We may even try to proselytize new converts feeling that if they believe, it will strengthen our own belief. But secretly we wonder why isn't it working for me? What am I missing? It is because we are not aware of the non-dual secret of living in the Kingdom.

How then could the early Christians sing while they let themselves be eaten by lions in the arena? They had a revelation of "Christ in you the hope of glory." [Colossians 1:27] We must admit, Christianity as it is taught today is not nearly as powerful. So they must have known something about Christianity that we don't know today.

THE ONE FALSE ASSUMPTION

Christianity isn't working for us because of this one small, but crucial assumption. The mind's concept of an objective entity, "me," inherently can never be truly one with what we imagine is another objective entity, "God." The dualistic mind can't manage it conceptually.

The false assumption that has created this barrier between us and God is the dualistic assumption that we are an individual body/mind and, we assume, so is God.

The only way past that is to see that the self we think we are doesn't, in fact, exist! And our only existence is in God who is Spirit and not an object or an objective entity. We have already looked for a self and couldn't find it. But maybe we won't be totally convinced until we find our "Real Self" in Christ. However, the problem is that our Real Self is not just another objective entity. It is no-thing. In other words it is not anything we can conceptualize, picture or think of. ("...Your real life is *hidden* in Christ with God" [Colossians 3:3 ESV]) Then there are these scriptures ... "If you cling to your life, you will lose it. But if you will give up your (conceptual) life for me, you will find it." [Matthew 10:39 NLT] "Whosoever shall seek to save his life shall lose it, and whosoever shall lose his life shall preserve it." [Luke 17:33]

THE MIND IS NOT YOURSELF THINKING!

You see, the mind is not an objective thing. It is just a process, the thinking process. So the mind doesn't really exist as an object or as anything. It is just thinking happening. "Mind" is just a noun used to describe a verb, an action. It is like "wind" used as a noun. Wind is not really an object. It is simply the air moving, an action. So the wind is only the blowing – not any "thing." The mind though thinks itself to be a thing, a "me," but is no one. It is just thoughts happening automatically stimulated by what is happening in the environment, memories, feelings, etc. But the mind is not a "me." It just thinks it is because of the way it works. The mind is not you thinking.

That is a result of the fall. Consciousness, your True Self, is what is aware of thoughts.

Let's see exactly what God has done to rectify this problem for us and precisely why we didn't understand this and probably weren't even told. We all know that "He died on the cross for us," but, more important, exactly how does that set us free and give us a new life? After all we still *feel* we are the same person as we were before we were a Christian.

EXERCISE #2
THE GREAT IMPOSTOR

Find three or four friends and ask them to do this experiment with you. You'll all have an interesting time.

Everyone stands in a circle.

1. Announce: "There is an impostor among us." Then read the next steps to the group.

2. Do you see anyone in the group who might be impersonating you?

3. What if someone looked exactly like you? Would you immediately know that person was an impostor?

4. Why?

5. So, the obvious conclusion is that anyone you can see, couldn't be you because you are who is *seeing* them. They are your objects. You (subject) are who is seeing them (object).

6. Now, close your eyes

7. Think of yourself. Say: "me."

8. Could this "me" you are seeing in thought be what you are?

9. Are you the "me" you see in thought or are you *what is seeing* the thought?

10. Should not the same hold true for thought as for sight?

11. So, the conclusion once again is, anyone you can see, even in thought, couldn't be you, because you are what is *seeing*. "Me" is your object. You (subject) are who is seeing "me" (as object).

12. Who then is the impostor?

13. Why then have you been living for this impostor, "me," all these years?

14. Can who is seeing the "me" *ever* be seen in thought? Of course not. Any self seen in thought would be your object, simply an observed thought or concept, thus not what you are as subject.

The learned, conditioned way of thinking of our self (as an object) may lead us to assume that this is simply nit-picking, mere sophistry. On the contrary, it reveals a very fundamental flaw in logic concerning our identity, one which is responsible for all our misery. Indeed it is responsible for all the suffering in the world, and is keeping us from a new life beyond our greatest imaginings and, most important, oneness with God.

CHAPTER 3: WHAT ARE WE THEN?

"There was the true Light coming into the world – genuine, perfect, steadfast Light – that illumines every person."
– [John 1:9 AB]

"That was the true light, which lighteth every man that cometh into the world." [John 1:9] What is this that "illumines every person" and the "True Light" that lighteth every person? This "True Light" doesn't just mean your conscience or that Jesus was a "good example" for us. Illumines means that the Spirit of Christ illuminates us with His consciousness, His awareness, His Spirit. It is the ability to be aware, conscious, sentient. That is, the pure, clear consciousness without content. Actually He *is* our bare, empty consciousness without thought. The largely unnoticed miracle of all miracles! Once recognized it is obvious and can never be forgotten, "whereby we cry 'Abba Father.'" [Romans 8:15] Others may disagree with you because they are seeing dualistically. But once one has clearly seen and recognized this it is undeniable.

Of course you as a separate individual are not God. There is no separate individual. He is your being, but the "mind" is neither His mind nor your mind. The mind at some point must also realize it is not you or yours either. It is just the thinking process, running on its own, affected by what's happening in the environment and/or in the belief system and worldview, etc. It's just cause and effect. If you "think" you are the mind, that is the problem. It is simply the thinking process we call mind, thinking it is a person, a "me."

The concept of self is tenacious. The mind often tricks us by imagining another self who sees this, behind the conceptual self. Then if we recognize that the mind is doing this, the mind just imagines yet another self which is knowing this. This can go on infinitely unless it is truly seen deeply that there really is no self *of any kind* and it is all an illusion of the mind. Then the "self" illusion will have no ground left to stand on.

"In Him Was Life and the Life was the Light of men." [John 1:4] This means our subjective sense of "I am" that we all have is the life of God i.e. the Spirit of Christ. It actually means that the Spirit of Christ is *our very light of consciousness,* our own sense of "I am." It's what makes us a sentient being.

You see, one of the problems with our worldview is that it isn't consciousness that appears in our body, as we have been told; it is *our body* that appears in consciousness, not to mention the entire universe. And consciousness is not a "thing" or anything phenomenally objective but noumenal Spirit i.e. Jesus is the "I am" of everyone. See if you can see this for yourself here and now. Could your body appear without consciousness? For that matter could *anything* appear without this miraculous consciousness *here*?

AT THE CRUCIFIXION

At the crucifixion, Jesus took our *self* (the body/mind we think we are) upon himself. "Since, therefore his children share in flesh and blood – that is, in the physical nature of human beings – he in a similar manner partook of the same nature, that by going through death He might bring to naught and make of no effect him who has the power of death, that is, the devil." [Hebrews 2:14, 15 AB] This happened in eternity as well as in time. "Who verily was foreordained before the foundation of the world, but was manifest in these last times for you." [1 Peter 1:20] "Jesus is the lamb slain from the foundation of the world." [Revelations 13:9]

This "I am" is our True Self, but it is not any "thing" such as the self we were looking for. It is not even an "it," being upstream of all thoughts and concepts. This "I am" is upstream of even "something" and "nothing," being the awareness in which they both appear. This is our bare sense of being.

If you don't understand it yet, pause a moment and look again for your self right now. Can you find a self as anything but thoughts and feelings? That's all there really is. We actually have no individual self. Only the sense of "I am." – Which is pure, empty consciousness without content. It is noumenal Spirit. Even thoughts and feelings do not belong to us, for there is no "me" causing them or to claim them! They come and go by themselves like the birds in the sky. Who we think we are is made of nothing but thoughts and concepts. No "thing" such as a self can actually be found. The miraculous sense of conscious awareness, "I am," is the same "I am" that spoke to Moses [Exodus 3:4]

Our very sense of being, "I am" *is* the Spirit of Christ! Please consider this. Moses asked the burning bush, "...when I come unto the children of Israel, and say unto them, the God of your fathers hath sent me unto you; and they shall say to me what is his name? What shall I say unto them?

And God said unto Moses, 'I am *that* I am...' " [Exodus 3:4] Doesn't this clearly mean that God was telling Moses that He was the very sense of "I am" that Moses had? "...and he said, thus shall you say unto the children of Israel, 'I am' hath sent me unto you." Now, that enigmatic scripture makes perfect sense doesn't it? Since one can find no other actual self, then the Spirit of Christ must be what-we-are in our deepest being, our sense of "I am," our pure awareness. This is what makes us aware and conscious. We are seeing the world through the eye of God. However, not knowing this, the mind has led us astray and hidden the Kingdom from us and given us a false identity as the body/mind, as "me," a separate being apart from all other beings and God.

YOU ARE NOT THE MIND

Nothing perceived can be what–you-are. In fact nothing perceived can be you or yours. The mind is not us or ours either, nor are emotions. Never look to emotions to tell you how you are. Mind is just a word to name the thinking process, not any "thing." You can see and observe thoughts so they can't be who is seeing them, but a part of the cause and effect phenomenal world. If you watch the mind carefully, over time, you will discover that it operates "by itself." Not by any "me." It is affected by the presence of the concept "me," but operates automatically on its own, just as our heart beats automatically. It is influenced by what is happening in the moment, by association with memories and habits, by our belief system, including our wants and fears that grew up around the false concept, self.

If you think you have any control over thoughts, just try to stop them, even for a few minutes. If you decide to rethink something it is not your will, it is because the thought to do so just appeared seemingly of itself. Please consider this: If your mind didn't actually operate by itself, if you really did have to decide to do something you would first have to *decide to decide*. But in order to do that you would have to *decide to decide to decide* and so on in an infinite regression. Proof the mind *must* operate spontaneously! The mind is neither you nor yours. This also means that "your" desires, fears, feelings and habits are not yours either.

What freedom when one sees this!

In fact, reading it in this book may trigger the action of watching your thoughts to see that they come of themselves by themselves.

EXERCISE #3
FREE AS A BIRD

1. Sit quietly and observe your thoughts as they appear. Stay objective and do not get caught up in them and forget what you are doing. Try to notice *how* they appear, and *from where.*

2. You will notice that they appear *before* you decide to think them. Your only "decision" may be to repeat them sub-vocally, and even that decision appears unbidden. It just seems as though you decided to think that thought because you think the thought is yours. Scientific experiments have proven that action is often initiated *before* a person is consciously aware they have even decided to act.

3. Now compare these "internal" observations with watching a bird as it flies across the sky. Did you bid it to appear? Did you claim ownership for the bird because it appeared? No, you just noticed it and allowed it to fly on.

4. If your thoughts appear unbidden, why do you claim ownership or control?

5. Do you try to stop the bird in flight because you don't want it there? No, because it is just part of the scenery, and by not feeling any sense of ownership you remain detached. The bird is simply one sight among many.

6. Can you see that as habitual thought patterns form around the illusory self they are triggered by association?

7. If you recognized that thoughts do not belong to the illusory self, or to any self, but were simply part of a cause and effect chain (as was the bird), wouldn't that remove the power of negative thoughts? You don't have to stop them: simply remaining detached removes their control. They are just part of the scenery.

CHAPTER 4: FROM HERE TO THERE AND BACK AGAIN

"God is ever present because He is the present."
– Author

I knew that my "self" was only thoughts, an illusion, but what was I really? Yes I had a personality and such, but that wasn't really a self, a me. I had an intuition that somehow this was where Jesus came in, but was unable to figure out how. This became a real dilemma for me. I had gotten this far, and did feel much freer, but I was left with nothing. I could find no other self and was at a loss as to what I was. One cannot take this lightly. It was an authentic case of "who can free me from this body of death?" I had assumed I had made a great discovery in seeing that my assumed self was a false self, just emptiness but I slowly sank into a "dark night of the soul." Caught firmly in this painful despair, I lived in this neither world too long.

However, at just that time I was corresponding with a friend who understood non-duality and he began to tell me about it. It took a while before I could understand, but as soon as I saw what he was getting at I realized that there were no "things-in-themselves." And that has made all the difference.

My friend was talking about the true sense of "I am" and how this "I am" was neither something nor nothing, but was prior to, or upstream of all conceptual thoughts such as self and other. I saw that this bare sense of being was the "light" of consciousness. We may also call it the sense of presence, here, now. This sense of "I am" is neither something nor nothing, but was the clear light of consciousness in which *all else appears*. I knew I was onto something. After much searching and pondering I was able to realize this deep knowing, this sense of "I am" cannot be denied and was actually the Spirit of Christ!

"I am crucified with Christ: nevertheless I live; *yet not I*, but Christ lives within me: and the life which I now live in the flesh I live by the *faith of the son of God* who loved me and gave himself for me." [Galatians 2:20] So, Christ is our actual life and it is by *His faith* we live. (That is, *not even by our own faith*, but His since there is no self to have faith!) We all share the same miraculous sense of "I am."

"For in Him we live, and move, and have our being." [Acts 17:28] We don't even know *how* we live and move and have our being, we just do it. It just happens! That gives us no alternative.

How do you move? How do you know "I am?" This is unique to life. No mechanical, computerized machine, no matter how sophisticated *will ever know the sense of "I am," consciousness, presence, being here, now.* This which knows I know.

There is no one but God, no self, no others and He is our very consciousness and our True Life. How else can it be? Now the important thing is, He is just our bare sense of "I am," pure consciousness without an object. But Christ is not our thoughts or feelings or our desires or fears nor even our mind. And, especially not *the false, separate, conceptual "me"* we always thought we were. That "me" is not Christ. Far from it. This is what the scripture means – "Whosoever shall seek to save his life (the conceptual self, 'me') shall lose it, and whosoever shall lose his life shall preserve it." [Luke 17:33] You must lose your (conceptual) life to find it (your non-conceptual life, the sense of "I am" in Jesus). Of course one cannot say "I am

Jesus" but we can say that the pure sense of "I am" is the Spirit of Christ.

By thoroughly seeing that "me" is just a concept, we lose it. It falls away of itself, like seeing how a magician's trick is done. It was just an illusion, an empty, dead, thought. Then over the months and years the old habits connected with it fade away as you mature as a Christian. "...be ye transformed by the renewing of your mind." [Romans 12:2]

All that appears, appears in the "I am" and only in the *now*. That's all there is. And all that is appearing is perceptions, "now." How the mind interprets the present stream of percepts is most important. These are the perceptions of seeing, hearing, tasting, touching, smelling and thinking. This appears as what we have always called *ourselves* and the *world*.

If we are living in the dualistic, fallen state, the mind interprets these senses as seer and seen, hearer and heard, taster and tasted, toucher and touched, smeller and smell, thinker and thought. This, simply, is dualism, dividing the subjective senses into objective things-in-themselves or our world model.

Yet there are no things-in-themselves actually, there are only perceptions appearing in consciousness. Non-dually there is only perceiving.

It is the conceptual mind that splits perceiving into perceiver and perceived. This becomes clearer with the renewing of the mind. You are one with what you are perceiving, phenomenally that is.

Thus, the dualistic mind is a *divided*-mind. It is divided-mind that creates the appearance and thus the belief in separate things-in-themselves. Such as, a table is known as a pre-existing thing-in-itself and the chair is another, separate, pre-existing thing-in-itself. In the "unfallen" or awakened awareness all is known as *a present flow of perceptions in consciousness*, not as many separate-things-in-themselves. Yes, even the body! This is the "real" the "solid" world believe it or not.

For instance, let's say you enter a restaurant and see the table, feel the knife and fork in your hand, smell the coffee in your cup, taste the food you are eating, hear the murmuring of the other patrons. And you *know* you are dining in a restaurant.

Yet none of that existed in itself. There is no seer and no table seen, simply seeing appearing in consciousness. No feeler and no knife and fork felt, simply feeling appearing in consciousness. No smeller and no coffee smelled, only smelling appearing in consciousness. No taster or food tasted, only tasting appearing in consciousness.

No hearer and patrons heard, only hearing appearing in consciousness.

It is the conceptual thought process then, that gives us the impression and thus the nearly unshakable belief in a pre-existing world composed of billions upon billions of separate, independent things-in-themselves, existing in space and time. As a child we didn't think dualistically and had to learn this dualistic world model from older people and gradually we stopped living in the Kingdom,[3] learned their dualistic conceptual worldview and left the Kingdom. We no longer live in the real world but in our thoughts about it!

Now, in these times, it is extremely rare for anyone to find their way back to the Kingdom by themselves. It goes against the dualistic logic and worldview we have learned, so we can't see our way out logically. We must make an intuitive leap, back upstream of, or prior to thoughts to *neither* something *nor* nothing and see it is all illuminated in conscious awareness, the "I am" of Jesus.

Does this sound insane and heretical? Actually dualism is the insanity and heresy. It is the world of the dead. At this point the reader will

---

3 We live in the Kingdom roughly up to three or as old as five years old.

either think it is all ridiculous and drop it because it doesn't fit their worldview or, if lucky, have at least enough courage to follow it through to understanding, especially if they sense the ring of truth whether they completely understand yet it or not.

Once this is understood many scriptures we have glossed over in the past as enigmatic will now jump out as very meaningful and profound. The Bible will open up for you.

AN EXAMPLE OF NONDUALITY

We have all experienced non-duality for ourselves, interpreted dualistically in our dreams. Our dream world seems just like our real world during the dream. That is until we awaken. Then it is obvious it was all just the *flow of perceptions* appearing in consciousness and nothing whatsoever was objective. The dream took up no space in our bedroom. That is how this dualistic world seems solid and real. Believe it or not, this waking life is the "Living Dream" as the old mystics have told us.

WHY DO WE HAVE A BODY?

The body is just a *point of view*, from which the world *including the body* can manifest by way of the five senses and the concept of space-time. It is a way to interact with phenomenality just as you do in a dream. How else could it be?

THE FIRST CHRISTIANS

The big question is, did the first Christians understand this? Of course! They were much more likely to understand than present day Christians. For example: "I do believe that there is considerable evidence that the first century teachings of Jesus carry forth a non-dualistic element. Generally, however, the near Second Temple Period, near eastern teachings of Jesus have been interpreted through a western, Aristotelian filter which is, of course, dualistic." – Dr Joseph Meador, PhD [4]

How then was this key revelation lost even though, as we have seen, there is a plethora of scriptures pointing to it?

It seems that the modern scholars haven't written much about this subject or how this most basic insight was lost. This is probably because the scholars didn't know about it themselves! And this is because this insight is NOT just intellectual

---

4 Dr Joseph Meador, MTh, PhD Professor of Religion and Dean, Southwest School of Bible Studies and Graduate School, Austin, Texas (Retired) (Personal correspondence)

knowledge. Rationality can take us only so far in this, the most important of insights.

As in all movements, especially young ones, some people join not so much because they understand and believe what the movement is about, but because they have a need to control things and be recognized as a key leader and, most important, control the wealth.

It is known that early in the new church different members in the scattered congregations began to compete for power and control. And those seeking power and control are not always the ones who have recognized "Christ in you, the hope of glory," [Colossians 1:27] but those who understood Christianity only from the dualistic point of view which robs it of much of its power.

And to keep it easier to control, these self-appointed leaders began to invent a hierarchy of different titles and positions such as Pope, Cardinal, Bishop, Priest, etc., in order to put them between God and the members. This is absolutely unnecessary if one truly sees Christ as their True Life. "But the anointing which ye have received from Him abideth in you, and ye need not that any man teach you: but as the same anointing teacheth you of all things, and is truth, and is no lie, and even as it hath taught you, ye shall abide in Him." [1 John 2:27]

As we know, anyone with this understanding needs no one to intercede with God for them. Isn't this true oneness with God?

THE GUIDANCE OF THE SPIRIT

If there is no individual self, then there can be no actual, effective volition. That's why volition only seems to work intermittently as the apostle Paul found out in Romans 7. What's the answer? Trust in, rely upon and stay with the " I am," the Spirit of Christ which we will discuss in the next chapter. We, as a conceptual self can neither do nor not do anything. (Not doing is just the negative form of doing.) The conceptual self cannot have an effective will or volition as it is just a thought *and a thought cannot think or do.* The Spirit of Christ will give us the urgings and actions as we trust in and rely upon the fact that we are in Him.

EXERCISE #4
IS CONSCIOUSNESS IN YOUR BODY?

We don't realize how deep our learned assumptions are embedded. Could all this really be a projection of consciousness? Is it really just a matter of how it has been interpreted? Dare we recognize that consciousness is not some quality or power that we "own" and exercise individually, and that *everything*, including our precious self, is nothing but consciousness?

Now, stand up with the book in your hand. Going only by what you see, here and now, not what you think or believe or remember ...

Look at your feet.
Now move your gaze up your body.
Look at your ankles,
your knees,
your hips,
stomach,
chest,
Can you see any further up your body?

Going by sight alone, not what you believe or feel, can you accurately describe what you *see* where your head is supposed to be?

We were taught that we are our body and that somehow, by some mysterious, unknown process, consciousness has appeared *in it.* We have assumed this for so long that we don't even question it. Isn't it time we looked to see for ourselves? Does consciousness appear in our body or is it *our body that appears in consciousness*?

See for yourself right now. Put down this book, look down at your body and ask yourself: "Is consciousness appearing in my body or is it my body that is appearing in this consciousness?" Don't go by your learned assumptions; just look openly and honestly, as if for the first time.

Then ask, "Could this body even appear without consciousness? Could *anything* appear without this consciousness here?"

What are we then? Are we our body as we have been told or are we consciousness, as we can *directly observe* for ourselves? So, what then *is* our body? Could it be consciousness also?

We think our conceptual self is everything we have and our conscious/awareness is nothing. Yet the conceptual self is nothing and conscious/awareness, "I am," is appearing as everything. This is because Jesus is all there is and He is the "being" of all that appears.

CHAPTER 5: THE ROMANS 7 SYNDROME

"As long as I am this or that,
I am not all things."
– Meister Eckhart

So now maybe we can crack the enigmatic "code" of Romans Chapters 7 & 8 and find out what that mysterious power is that makes us "do what we hate." Here is a great secret which very few recognize and almost no one teaches. But it makes all the difference in the world when it comes to our Christian life.

(First, look for a "self" again, and remember the Self Chart and the Imposter Exercise we did earlier.)

Two Bible verses to keep in mind as you read this chapter:

1. "For the law is the strength of sin"
[1 Corinthians 15:56]

2. "The law is for the lawless"
[1 Timothy 1:9]

This is an explanation of those key passages in Romans 7 that so puzzled this author in the beginning.

In italics are the actual margin notes I wrote in my Bible as I finally recognized what the passages meant.

Romans 7:8 AB: "But sin, finding opportunity in the commandment [to express itself] got a hold on me and aroused and stimulated all kinds of forbidden desires (lust, covetousness). For without the law sin is dead – the sense of it is inactive and a lifeless thing."

By relying on our supposed self's volition we awaken and activate the desires and fears associated with the false conceptual self.

Romans 7:15 AB: "For I do not understand my own actions – I am baffled, bewildered. I do not practice or accomplish what I wish, but do the very thing I loathe [which my moral instinct condemns]."

Because the conceptual self, being merely a thought, can have no effective volition or power, I don't do what I should do, and what I want to do. But do what I should not do. What I do is dictated by the desires and fears accumulated through the belief in the conceptual self.

Romans 7:17 AB: "However, it is no longer I who do the deed, but the sin [principle] which is at home in me and has possession of me."

It is not I who does the deed, but the desires and fears connected to the self concept. They possess me when I try to follow the laws.

Trying to use our self's illusory volition to follow the law, identifies us with the conceptual self and affirms the conceptual self thereby arousing and activating the needs and desires it is linked with, giving them power. The result is "what I would do that I do not; but what I hate that I do" [Romans 7:15.]

The secret is to just see that there is no "me." The conceptual self is neither doing nor not doing any of it! It's all just happening spontaneously. Nothing I do is "me" or "mine" or "my" doing. Since I now understand I literally can do nothing of my conceptual self, I can now relax and trust my actions to the Spirit of Christ! (My sense of "I am") This is also known as "non-volitional living."

This doesn't mean that you will live perfectly and sin free from now on. Old habits connected to the "me" may still operate. But there is forgiveness for these and that helps keep us from relying on the illusory volition of the conceptual self. So they will subside. You will "...be transformed by the renewing of the mind." [Romans 12:2] If not, then your understanding needs to be deepened and more complete.

EXERCISE #5
THE CUP AND LIGHT EXPERIMENT

Do this experiment in the evening or in a darkened room. Situate yourself at a table and use a flashlight with the room lights out. Read through the assignment once and then do it. The intellectual understanding is not nearly as important as the experiential, intuitive insight.

1. Place an ordinary cup on the table and sit down with it in front of you.

2. Just look at the cup for a moment. Notice its shape, color, texture, size, and distance from you.

3. You would ordinarily say that you are seeing a cup, but let's see if that is so. Turn the light out. Now, can you see the cup?

4. Without the light, could a cup appear?

5. What has actually been removed, the cup or the light?

6. If only the light has been removed and the cup does not appear, what were you really seeing? A cup, or light appearing as a cup?

7. Next, turn the light back on. What do you notice? A cup and a table or light appearing as a cup and a table? Even though you know intellectually that you are only seeing light waves appearing as a cup, your conditioned way of thinking still probably insists on labeling this "one" light as different things, a cup, a table, etc. This is because the mind is conditioned to habitually focus on the *forms* and not the *light.*

8. Next we are going to notice another kind of light: the "Spiritual Light" of Consciousness in which there is awareness of even the physical light and the forms that it takes. Cup your hands around your eyes as though you were looking through binoculars and look through them at the cup. Notice the cup that appears at the other end.

9. Notice the *absence of any kind of appearance here at the end nearest you.* This is pure awareness or the "Light of Consciousness." Without the "Light" at the near end could a cup

appear at the other end ? Compare this experiment with steps 6 and 7.

10. *What are you really seeing?* A physical cup, phenomenal light or “Light” (Consciousness) appearing as a cup?

CHAPTER 6: WALKING AFTER THE SPIRIT

"The eye with which I see God
is the same eye with which He sees me."
– Meister Eckhart
14th Century Christian Mystic

Romans 7:18 "For I know that in me (that is, in my flesh), dwelleth no good thing: For to will is present with me; but how to perform that which is good I find not."

As we discovered in the last chapter, *"In my flesh" means "my conceptual self." This means that volition is an illusion and doesn't work because the conceptual self cannot do anything being only a concept. However the self concept does attract desires and fears associated with the "me" which do affect our belief system which then leads to automatic re-actions which are self centered. By seeing that our concept of self is an illusion, a mere idea, the desires and fears associated with it are not aroused or automatically activated.*

THIS, THEN, IS "WALKING AFTER THE SPIRIT"

"There is therefore now no condemnation (no guilt imputed) to them which are *in Christ Jesus, who walk (identify) not after the flesh (the conceptual, body self) but after the spirit (the sense of 'I am').* For the law of the spirit of life in Christ Jesus hath made me *free* from the law of sin and death (identity with self). For that which the law (what you think you should or shouldn't do) could not do, and that it was weak through the flesh (no effective volition), God sending his own Son in the likeness of sinful flesh (as a body/mind), and for sin, condemned sin in the flesh (exposed the conceptual self): that the righteousness of the law might be fulfilled in us, who walk (identify) not after the flesh (conceptual 'me'), but after the Spirit ('I am')." [Romans 8:1-4]

In other words let your life be lived by the "I am," the Spirit of Christ.

WHAT WALKING AFTER THE SPIRIT IS NOT

It is not "killing the ego" or "dying to the flesh." It is simply seeing through the illusion of the conceptual self. Then it will begin to dissolve on its own. Self oriented habits may linger on for a while, but the clearer you see the sooner they subside.

The more you try to "die to self" the more you will activate the desires and fears connected to the conceptual self. After all, who dies to self? Is there yet another self? And the more powerful will be the urge to sin. In other words the harder we try the worse it gets.[5] But that does not mean to give in to sin, but realize it is of the conceptual self and not you or yours and rely on the Spirit. You neither resist nor give in. It is neither law nor license. But trust in, rely on and identify with the sense of "I am" ... the Spirit of Christ.

NEITHER LAW NOR LICENSE

Walking after the Spirit is neither following laws nor giving in to license. We've already found that that doesn't work.

Remember there is no real "me," so that rules out anyone to do either. So what is happening? Since the belief system was built upon a false, "me," it has many needs, fears and desires connected with it so we automatically, habitually react to situations from those beliefs. But if we can understand that those thoughts and feelings aren't our needs, fears and desires and rely on Christ, it allows the Spirit of "Christ in you" to act instead.

---

5 How many ministers have been caught doing the very things they preach against? This is why.

As time goes by those automatic, habitual reactions die out and the body reacts less and less from those thoughts and feelings and acts (instead of reacts) from the pure "I am." Recognizing what-we-are can't be just an intellectual assent but must be a deep life changing insight that is forever imprinted on the mind, where we, as a "self," are left no ground to stand on.

THE BODY/MIND'S THOUGHTS AND FEELINGS ARE NOT YOU OR YOURS

Once again, we are taught that thoughts and feelings are ours and we identify with them as what we are. However, in the Imposter Exercise we learned that anything we can see couldn't be us or ours because, like an eye cannot see itself, what we "see" can't be what is seeing and a thought can't think.

Thoughts come and go automatically by themselves. It may take weeks or even months of watching thoughts before one is totally convinced of this, but it is well worth it. We may believe it is us who decides what to think, but that thought to deliberately think of something also is automatic. And as for feelings, no one needs to tell us how hard it is to control them. The attempt to watch thoughts and feelings may well be triggered by what you are reading here.

However, we need to recognize, or re-cognize, that they are not us or ours but just a big bundle of habits, desires and fears which lead to reacting automatically to what's going on in our environment. We are simply the awareness of them. They have *nothing* to do with our actual Life, the pure, still light of Christ in which all is appearing and being.

Can we see how liberating this is? If we can see this it instantly frees us from their pain and control. We can't claim the good thoughts and feelings either, least we identify with all thoughts and feelings.

This doesn't mean we should act like an unfeeling robot. As a matter of fact, try it. You can't. However, knowing that the mind is apart from what-you-are, you can be free of its control. You will then begin to experience the "renewing of the mind" [Romans 12:2].

The more one stays in this "magical now," the more likely the recognition will happen. This is because one is focused on real life rather than concepts, imagination and memories. There really is only now. It's the same now you knew and lived in as a child. Now is the doorway to the Kingdom of Heaven.

"There exists only the present instant...
a Now which always and
without end is itself new.
There is no yesterday nor any tomorrow,
but only Now, as it was a thousand years ago
and as it will be a thousand years hence."
– Meister Eckhart,
14th Century Christian Mystic

EXERCISE # 6
THE NOW EXPERIMENT

The *here and now* is the entrance to the Kingdom of Heaven. (If possible, have someone slowly read this to you. Spend time with each sense.)

Without personalizing or judging anything try the following exercise:

If thoughts carry you off, as soon as you notice them, don't fight them, simply ignore them and return to the now.

First, *listen*. What sounds are you hearing? It may be traffic outside, voices in the next room, a radio in the distance, the sounds of nature. The point is to notice every nuance of sound.

Second, *feel*. Start with your feet and move up your body. Notice what your shoes feel like, the feel of the chair under you, your arms and hands, your neck, head, face, the feel of your clothing on your body.

Third, *see*. Notice the room about you, any movement, objects. Take it all in. What's happening?

Fourth, *smell*. Is there a scent in the air?

Fifth, *taste*. Is there a taste in your mouth?

Say the word "now" to yourself. Be in it.
Stay here awhile and just *be*.

We have probably noticed all these things before in bits and pieces, but we rarely put them all together. If we really notice any of these things it is in brief snatches between other thoughts of this and that.

Did you perhaps relax just a bit as you were doing the experiment? Maybe you noticed your neck and shoulder muscles loosened. You might have found that anxieties lessened and disturbing thoughts ceased to intrude for a brief spell. If you happen to be outdoors it will probably enhance the effect. Being in nature seems to expand our awareness.

Try to do this experiment as often as you can remember during the day. You will begin to notice something magical, a familiar specialness. It is a point of contact with *life* in the purest sense of the word. It may take a while to generate this contact, especially if you are in a tense emotional state, but keep it up. There is more *here* than we have first assumed.

After doing the Now Experiment, consider these questions:

1. Where do you spend most of your *mental life*?

   a. Thoughts of past events, rethinking them – 1 to 100% of the time
   b. Imaginations of future events, anticipating – 1 to 100%
   c. The present moment, living now – 1 to 100%

2. Which is most real: a, b, or c?

3. Could you be missing your real life?

4. Why? (Are you trying to rationalize the past, anticipate the future?)

5. Where does most of your mental strain come from: past, future or present?

6. Which do you prefer: a, b, or c? Why?

7. How can you live more consistently in the present?

8. Explain: All there is, is NOW!

NOTE: Gain release from fears about the future by noticing that "right now, at this moment I am okay." And recognize that your actual self, in Christ, is always okay and is invulnerable. In any case, fears are not yours because you are what is seeing them. Your True Life never has fear.

CHAPTER 7: LIVE GLADLY

"For my yoke is easy and my burden is light."
– Matthew 11:30

We think we want the truth, but then we look for it only where we want it to be. This is like the old story about the man crawling around on his hands and knees under a street light. Someone comes by and asks him what he is doing.

"I'm looking for the twenty dollar bill I dropped," he replies.

"You lost it here?" the passerby asks, looking around.

"No," the man says, "I lost it down there somewhere," pointing down the darkened street.

"Then why on earth are you looking for it here?"

"Because the light is much better here," he replies.

We can also confuse spiritual feelings with spirituality, mystical feelings with mysticism, and holy feelings with holiness. Nor is simply acting spiritual being spiritual, acting mystical being mystical, or acting holy being holy.

Change will happen by itself, not by trying. *The manifestation of the fruit of the spirit* is what will happen: love, joy, peace, patience, gentleness, goodness, faith, meekness, self control. [Galatians 5:22, 23]

WHY IS THIS BOOK DIFFERENT?

Why is this book different from others you may have read in the past? Unlike the books which tell us what to do and what to believe, the recognition of what-we-are in Christ actually transforms us in an instant and will never be lost or forgotten once clearly seen. As the real meaning of what we have glimpsed sinks into our heart and mind over the next minutes, days and years we will effortlessly change inwardly and probably outwardly as the fruit of the spirit manifests while understanding grows.

If being a Christian seems difficult, then we have missed the main point. Unlike a philosophy or doctrine, one doesn't have to remember rules, behavior codes or even how to apply them in a particular situation. We don't have to know the "practical application" of conduct or psychological guidelines or any so called "truths" or perform any rituals. We just need to know the "I am." This will guide us into all truth.

In fact we don't have to do anything after we recognize or re-cognize what-we-are. This recognition points to the fact that volition is a myth just as much as the self is a myth. The very ground is cut from under us and we fall into the arms of Jesus.

When Jesus uttered "it is finished" from the cross [John 19:30] he also meant any effort on your part is also finished. *Tetelestai* is the Greek word for finished; a bill that has been paid in full, completed, no more effort is required of us. In fact we have no actual ability to do or not to do of our will or volition. The truth is we never did. When we actually did do what we know we should do it was happenstance. We were simply following a lifetime of conditioning and when we fail to live up to our so-called volition or willpower it is a vain futility, a useless, ineffective attempt to violate cause and effect, for volition is a myth. But we believe in volition because it comes into our mind to do something and then we do it, except when it is not in accord with our urges.

We are told to "just try harder" and when we do we employ the concept of the "me," who we think we are as the "doer." In doing so we awaken and energize and give power to the conditioned habits engrained in the idea of "me." That includes all its lifelong acquired needs, longings, desires, fears, habits and hatreds.

And that is what happens.

Our actions follow our most powerful habits and desires, mitigated only by our strongest fears of exposure or punishment for either the physical body or self image or both. The results will be a vain disappointment. *For if volition really worked wouldn't we all be able to live the perfect life we want to?*

Instead, when we truly recognize what-we-are we know at that moment that what we have been looking for is simply what is looking. And that is the miracle of miracles. "This" is the source and substance of *all* that appears in the universe throughout eternity! "... The worlds were framed by the word of God, so that *things which are seen were not made of things which do appear.*" [Hebrews 11:3]

We are then assured that the moment we glimpse the sense of "I am" and see it as "Christ our life" we will enter into rest. "So you have not received the spirit of fear, but ye received the spirit of adoption, whereby we cry 'Abba, Father'" [Romans 8:15] And we will never again have a question about our salvation so sure and solid it will be.

THE DOUBLE SLIT EXPERIMENT

The double-slit experiment[6] has confirmed the undeniable role of consciousness in the manifestation of phenomenality. The experiment begins by firing streams of photons from a single source through two vertical slits arranged side by side in a barrier. On the other side of this barrier is a screen that can record (show) where each photon arrives. The result is an interference fringe pattern on the screen which appears as a series of light and dark vertical stripes, the type you would expect when two waves meet in a river. However, when a *single* photon passes through the slits and reaches the screen it *still* forms an interference fringe pattern on the screen *as if it interfered with itself.*

The interference fringe pattern shows that the light has traveled as if it were ripples or waves radiating out from the single source in expanding circles as when a rock is dropped into a pond. The light waves move through both slits at once, forming *two* circular wave patterns on the other side of the barrier, radiating out from each of the

---

6 See John Gribbin's *Schrodinger's Kittens and the search for reality*, and Michael Talbot's *Beyond the Quantum*, for good explanations of this and other recent experiments.

two slits. When these two circular waves of light reach the screen they interfere with each other just as when two expanding circles of water wave patterns meet, canceling the wave in one place where a peak and a trough meet and enlarging it in another place where two peaks or two troughs meet. This is what causes the series of light and dark vertical stripes called an interference pattern.

A simple version of this experiment was originally performed by Thomas Young early in the nineteenth century to "prove" that light was a wave, not a particle as Isaac Newton believed. Of course it is now accepted that either wave or particle behavior is manifested according to the type of experiment performed.

A NEW VERSION OF THE DOUBLE SLIT EXPERIMENT

In 1983 the experiment was taken further using single electrons instead of photons and it was found that if only one electron at a time is sent, the interference pattern *still forms.* As the individual electrons strike the screen they build up to form the same interference pattern as the photons did. It is as though each individual electron went through *both* slits in the barrier at the same time and interfered with itself! That is the only way the interference pattern could still appear. This means that the electron must start as a particle, but disappear and "travel" as a *wave of probabilities* and then reappear at the screen as a particle once again.

Now that seems strange enough, but the really amazing part is that if you try to check or monitor the two slits with instruments to observe which one (or both) of the slits the electron actually travels through, the wave becomes an individual electron particle again at the slit where it was detected and *the interference pattern disappears*! This had also been found to be true for photons.

The act of observing actually caused the electron to manifest. Before that it didn't actually exist as a particle, there were only statistical probabilities of where it might be. The electron, by becoming a particle at the slits because it was "looked at," stops being a probability wave and must then "choose" which slit it will travel through. Thus, it no longer interferes with itself and the interference pattern no longer forms. This experiment has since been performed using whole sodium atoms with the same results.

Physicists, in trying to establish the reality of the reductionists' world of matter, have succeeded in proving the opposite. Nothing is anything in itself, but gets its meaning through relationships with everything else. And, to their puzzlement, that requires consciousness.

"Matter is derived from consciousness, not consciousness from matter."
– Sir James Jeans Noted British Scientist

LIVING IN THE KINGDOM

We are actually transformed and elevated to a higher dimension to enter into rest in the Kingdom of God.

"Labor to enter into rest" [Hebrews 4:11]

What is living at rest like?

Living at rest: As a symbol of rest the priests in the old temple in Jerusalem wore linen clothes to symbolize a lack of perspiration which represented effort or work. A lack of perspiration symbolized rest.

In the fall, Adam was doomed to "live by the sweat of your brow you shall eat." [Genesis 3:17-19] This is because he had acquired a false, conceptual self with a conceptual will or personal volition. This meant having to do things he was not disposed to do in order to survive. If he had not fallen and acquired the body/self concept, he wouldn't have seen anything as toil but as just "being" and would have been disposed to act as necessary. Thus it would not be an effort even if it did require physical energy. One might contrast it to changing a flat tire as compared to the energy involved in your favorite sport or activity. The former is an effort and the latter is a pleasure.

Do this and get God's blessing

We have been told by some Bible teachers that we must do something for God in order to get something from Him. It's like, "Jump through this hoop and get this treat." Actually it is completely the opposite. We don't "do" in order to have, we "do" because we have the Spirit of Christ.

He took away the penalty for sins that are prompted by the self concept and gave us His own being as our conscious awareness. When we find out what He has already done for us, we are transformed spontaneously. And, as our understanding deepens we are further transformed without effort or even thought. "Be ye transformed by the renewing of the mind." [Romans 12:2]

Do self improvement programs help?

There is a never ending flow of all kinds of self improvement programs. We have all tried them before. The reason they don't really work is revealed by their very label, *self improvement* program. What self do we improve? We have seen in chapter 5 the harder we attempt to utilize the conceptual self's volition, the more we end up doing the opposite of what we want. We have discovered that relying on this false self stirs up the same old wants, lusts, fears and etc. And this takes over control of the body and mind.

THE SERMON ON THE MOUNT

The Sermon on the Mount [Matthew 6:25-34] sounds very reassuring, but is it really practical? The answer is; not unless one has recognized that their "True Life is hidden with Christ in God" and has entered into rest. Otherwise, one will be anxious about taking care of themselves and their family, etc. It is too easily misunderstood as not needing to work or a license for laziness. But "walking after the Spirit" takes the "work" out of work. It is printed here for your inspiration.

> Therefore I say unto you, take no thought for your life, what ye shall eat, or what ye shall drink; nor yet for your body, what ye shall put on. Is not the life more than meat, and the body than raiment?
>
> Behold the fowls of the air: for they sow not, neither do they reap, nor gather into barns; yet your heavenly Father feedeth them. Are ye not much better than they?

Which of you by taking thought can add one cubit unto his stature?
And why take ye thought for raiment? Consider the lilies of the field, how they grow; they toil not, neither do they spin:
And yet I say unto you, That even Solomon in all his glory was not arrayed like one of these.
Wherefore, if God so clothe the grass of the field, which today is, and tomorrow is cast into the oven, shall he not much more clothe you, O ye of little faith?
Therefore take no thought, saying what shall we eat? Or, what shall we drink, or, wherewithal shall we be clothed?
(For after all these things do the Gentiles seek:) for your heavenly Father knoweth that ye have need of all these things.
But seek ye first the Kingdom of God, and his righteousness; and all these things shall be added unto you.
Take therefore no thought for the morrow; for the morrow shall take thought for the things of itself. Sufficient unto the day is the evil thereof.

NON-VOLITIONAL LIVING

We have now discovered that resisting the self's needs activates them, while not resisting them makes them stronger. Doesn't this illustrate perfectly that *neither* doing nor not-doing is the only answer? Non-volition is the way out – the *only* way out. And, thank goodness it isn't something we must *do*. You have been removed from the situation by discovering that there isn't a "you" to do anything. Non-volitional living is simply realizing that *right now, at this moment, you are neither doing nor not-doing*. And if it seems "you" are doing, it is merely a habitual assumption. Doing just happens. It is simply the Reality, here now. Realizing non-volitional living cuts off every option the thought process believes it had. Everything is being taken care of. It is finished. Rest. That is all that is possible.

FREE WILL OR PREDESTINATION?

"In whom also we have obtained an inheritance, being predestined according to the purpose of Him who worketh all things according to the council of His own will." [Ephesians 1:11]

"It is in Christ that we found out who we are and what we are living for. Long before we first heard of Christ and got our hopes up, He had his eye on us for glorious living, part of the overall purpose He is working out in everything and everyone." [Ephesians 1:11 MSG]

For ages there has been much spirited debate by scholars, philosophers and theologians over the question of whether man has free will or is subject to predestination (determinism). The joke is that it is neither. For they too have fallen for the illusion of being an object, an entity, a self. Few ever think to even question it. If there is no self then who is there to have free will? Or, for that matter, who is there to be controlled by determinism? But the debate rages like children arguing amongst themselves over whether the monster is in the closet or under the bed. Usually free will has the consensus, not because it can be proven but, well, if *feels* like we have free will. And anyhow the alternative – determinism – really amounts to fatalism and who wants that?

If the thought process is identified with a conceptual self (as it is for most of the world) then belief in free will is necessary for laws and values to have any restraint at all on people's actions (through punishment and reward). If determinism was the prevalent belief then there would be little social control, more chaos and anarchy. (Though the current trend to be a victim and blame circumstances and inanimate things seems to be leading us in that direction.)

While we live with the identification with the conceptual self, it will seem like we have free will (though it seems oddly capricious and intermittent). Then, when the identification with the conceptual self actually evaporates, both interdependent concepts of free will and determinism fall away because there is neither a self nor a no-self to be subject to either. What-we-are is "upstream" or prior to all such dualities (even space-time). True life and true actions originate from here.

Everything happens as it must. It always has. Divine spontaneity then opens to "I just *am*."

HOW DO I SHARE THIS WITH OTHERS?

First, a person has to want to understand this. It is not something one can talk or argue someone into. It takes that moment of spiritual recognition to really understand. Most of all you must have had the recognition yourself. Then, if you are ready to share, people will come to you. When you feel they are sincere, you can share and recommend this book.

Something that I believe helped this author when I was a struggling Christian was that I wanted to know God for who He is regardless of whether it was of any personal benefit to me or not. That excludes doing it for the self.

It may take several readings of this book before your understanding is opened. Your own mindset, due to your worldview and the dualistic thought process, will blind you from even considering much of what you've read. Indeed, this truth is not understood by the intellect only. It takes a leap of spiritual intuition, a moment of spiritual insight to "see the Light." One cannot make this happen. It comes only by the grace of God. One can only hear (read) this "Good News" and stay in this attitude while it works within you to open your mind for the transmission of the insight.

There are various ways to be open. One way is to dwell on the pure sense of "I am" as much as possible every spare moment. You can even say "I am" sub-vocally to yourself.

This sense of "I am" is the Spirit of God. But because it has no other qualities except Pure Awareness, we look to what we are aware *of* rather than this clear, pure, still space "here." (Where we think our head is.)

Notice the great miracle that is occurring spontaneously here and now. The world, thoughts and feelings are spontaneously appearing here, now. We don't know how.

THE TRUE MEANING OF "REPENT"

In the beginning of this book the reader was told that it wasn't about gaining something, but about losing something, the illusions that hid what is already within you. For you see we have been looking in the wrong direction and for the wrong thing. So instead of looking at thoughts and feelings, we found we must turn our gaze around and look deep within. This action is translated as "repent"[7] (which actually means "beyond or upstream of thoughts, concepts and feelings) in the Bible. So, we find that entering the Kingdom is not accomplished by doing anything but by simply recognizing what God has already done for us. So it's not what we gain, but what we lose that counts.

As one continues to appreciate this Awareness "here" it builds within you until one day when you aren't even expecting it, the revelation of this miraculous Light of Being, deep within, will dawn and you will know the truth... and this will make you free.

LIVING IN THE SPIRIT

Walking after the Spirit doesn't take learning a bunch of truths and remembering to apply and use them. All problems can be seen to originate and come from the delusion of an objective, volitional self. Once that is seen, all the other "truths" flow

---

7 Repent, μετανοεω, **μετα** = beyond, **νοεω** = thoughts, concepts, feelings.

out of that. Here are some examples of the bits of wisdom that will come to you as you live "in the Spirit."

Emotions are not bad in themselves. They can be wonderful. It is just that when we identify with them as us or ours, they are in control. See them as you would see a beautiful painting (or a bad one). Not as you or yours. If we recognize them for what they are, as something we are perceiving and thus, not us or ours, we can let them come and go...like the clouds. There is then no need to fight against them, which just makes them stronger and more in control, or to try and hold onto them which warps and perverts them.

When we identify with emotions, we will slavishly do things for them and because of them - trying to get and keep the good emotions and to avoid and get rid of the bad ones. This only gives them power and control over us. It is a losing battle and causes the opposite effect. Inner peace is the quiet detachment from them as you are with a bird as it passes unbidden and un-owned across the clear blue sky.

In some cases emotions are not related to some causal factor in the environment and may be organic, such as chronic depression. If walking after the Spirit doesn't mitigate it, consult your physician.

Emotions - Purified of ownership and attachment can be useful as originally intended to reliably warn us when others or situations are not right or are dangerous and also when they are good and right. Otherwise, others can easily manipulate and use us through our ego needs, our self doubts, fears and desires.

Fame - People want fame because they sense that they are no-one and think that if many other people know and admire them, then that will make them someone real, someone of worth. But when it doesn't work they feel even worse.

Fortune - If you haven't already found out how to be happy in the moment, then fortune will not bring you happiness.

Crisis people get attention and it makes them feel important. They secretly feel they are nobody and their lives are dull and boring. Crisis makes them feel like somebody who has important things to attend to.

Teenage Rebellion - Teenagers have come to an age when they realize down deeply, unconsciously that the conceptual self is really no-one. It scares them and they try to affect an identity. They copy attitudes, beliefs, affectations and dress from others in order to try to be somebody. In their unhappiness and lostness and because they are frustrated when they can't have everything they want or do what they want, they blame "society" for their fear and frustration. As though "society" was an entity who was being unfair to them.

Happiness - List all the things you personally think you need to get, or to get rid of in order to be happy. Then see how almost all of them are a product or need of the conceptual self. Thus it will be clear why you don't need them and always have had everything you need and more.

The body and brain - We should view them not as what-we-are, but the way consciousness (what-we-are) manifests phenomenally. We have been taught that it is the brain that somehow creates consciousness, but that is the opposite of the reality. The body and brain are manifested using conceptual space/time and thus are temporary. Consciousness is "upstream" or prior to space/time and is non-temporal or what is incorrectly called eternal. Thinking is temporal, that is, thinking manifest via time and is a function of the brain. The brain is what thinks, but it is consciousness that *perceives* the thoughts and *knows* that they are happening. Consciousness does not think, it illuminates (makes visible) what the brain is doing.

Being - The only thing we have to “do” is to just *be*. And that happens without effort. Anything else and we fall into delusion. This will sound very strange and confusing until it actually happens in experience. Then it becomes clear that this is all one has ever done.

Love of detachment - Most people think that love is required or owed in return for one’s own love. But real love requires nothing from the other person. Not because you don’t care about them, but because you require nothing from them. We think we must change those we love so that they will treat us the way we want them to treat us. But that is not love. We can’t love them for our own fulfillment. That never works. When we recognize what-we-are, we will see that we are already fulfilled, we need nothing and we can’t gain or lose anything and nothing whatsoever can actually harm us. That is the "I am," the true core of our being.

Ambition vs Living in the Moment Not living *for* the moment but *in* it. Just being. Some will try to exploit this to use for their own self indulgence. They will use it to become self-absorbed.

Happily explore the Kingdom of Heaven with friends. First find understanding yourself, then you can have weekly or monthly get-togethers with friends and do the Experiments from this book.

We feel we need to be somebody and that we need to have opinions. But what we actually do is copy from other people's personalities and adopt their second-hand opinions. It is okay to not have a personality and to not have an opinion. You can't really see your own personality very well, so you jump to the conclusion that you don't have one and adapt someone else's.

Helping others - You cannot really help others if you are just helping them because you think you should out of guilt. When you have those "good intentions" you can end up causing more harm than good. This is because it is an act of "intentional" volition and most likely misguided.

When you spontaneously help someone without the intention of being good it will more likely be successful.

Try putting a small "C" for "consciousness" on the back of your left hand by your watch. Let it remind you to take the perspective of consciousness (the watching) rather than the thinker and notice that "I am looking from pure consciousness." Everything perceived appears in consciousness, is consciousness and consciousness is the Spirit of Christ.

Walking after the spirit is not just not doing anything. Nor is it doing anything you want. It is where doing happens spontaneously and appropriately without deliberation. There is no doer nor anything or anyone who has been "done to."

No-self means no volition. Not doing is still volition. It is just the negative aspect of volition. Non-volition is the absence of both doing and not doing.

The fear of no-self. You cannot experience your "True Being" while the thought process and belief system cling to the illusion of the individual self.

The "True Self" seems impossibly subtle while the illusory self seems so concrete. But that's the view while in the delusion. Actually the opposite is true.

Never turn your mind or will over to someone else no matter how much you trust or admire or fear them - especially if they are trying to use the authority of God. Not even if it is for some good cause, such as a religious or charitable group. Always test what they tell you with the reality of the Kingdom here and now and your own experience, not just with the doctrines or theories you may have adopted.

It is useless to go looking for excitement or diversion. That has been your problem. It can't be your answer. There is plenty of wonder in exploring what is right *here, now.*

Never try to share spiritual knowledge above your present level of experience.

All spiritual knowledge should come from and be verified in your own actual day to day experience. Never accept a teaching until you have tested it in your own experience and verified it with what you have already proven in this manner. Not even if it seems to come right from God.

It is perfectly all right to investigate any teaching or theory if you do it with this kind of care and verification. But just because it seems supernatural or obvious doesn't mean it is what it appears to be.

"I am" is not a thought, not happening to any "me." Not the thoughts of anyone. "I am" is the actuality, but not the thinker. You don't have to be anyone - you never were.

Spontaneous action - Only the sense of being the doer is the problem. It is caused by identification with a "me" concept. Everything is movement in consciousness. It doesn't involve a "me." It is witness-ing what is happening. It is only what *knows* what is happening. What you are doing at this moment is what is destined. Enjoy fulfilling your destiny.

Notice the decision to watch your thoughts to see if they actually do appear spontaneously. This decision also happened by itself or was triggered by a related thought. See how thoughts just appear, as well as decisions also. Mind goes its own way.

Your present emotion is *not how you are.* You are the *knowing*...or what knows about the emotion. You are what knows you know...the pure light. This is not affected by anything.

Linear mind becomes conditioned with habitual thought processes. But seeing the whole is a different kind of process - non-linear. Linear thought is like reading a description of a picture while non-linear is like actually seeing the whole picture at once.

How to stay on track - Trying to fix up and satisfy the self is "doing in order to have" and is a never ending treadmill. Your True Self is already perfect and at peace.

"No other animal searches for the truth. We do." – Edmund Bolles.

See the body/brain as where thinking is done and how we interact with the world. The body/brain is what appears in Consciousness, not the origin of consciousness.

Everything that appears is consciousness, and this is not any "thing."

Trying to always get what you want or think you have a right to blinds you to what you really have already (not just materially) and what you can really get. Volition is the problem.

The Sabbath represents Walking after the Spirit and living at rest!

The "Word" created the world. Words are conceptual. Concepts create the illusion of things-in-themselves, the world of things.

When Jesus was crucified the big, thick, heavy curtain, the veil, between the Holy of Holies and the sanctuary in the old temple was torn apart. Two cherubs were pictured on it representing the veil of flesh, dualistic thought which is barring the way to the Holy of Holies.

The eternal now is non-linear and simultaneous. Space-time is a concept used to extend the now to produce the appearance of phenomenality and linear time.

Opposite concepts are interdependent and at the same time mutually exclusive. Opposites allow conceptualizing and conceptualizing gives us the mistaken belief in separate things - or things-in-themselves. But it is all built on non-material percepts spontaneously arising in consciousness.

A truly "awakened" person may seem disappointingly unremarkable. However, many are seeking awakening only in order to appear as someone special. This is contrary to the understanding and so discourages them. No affectations are necessary.

Thinking is actually not necessary, believe it or not. Walking after the Spirit will give you the proper urges when acting and speaking.

Why certain things are repeated in this book. It is because they are hard to understand deeply and need to be approached from many different directions.

Return to the here-and-now, not doctrines, not spirituality, not even religion. But what is discoverable in the here and now by honestly looking at the here and now and being willing to re-examine your most basic assumptions and most cherished opinions. Discovering our Life in Christ is a never-ending joy.

An age of awakening in the Kingdom of Heaven is upon us!

ABOUT THE AUTHOR

Galen Sharp is a non-dual author who has studied the Bible in depth over the course of his life. His exploration of the Bible from the non-dual perspective was the key to a radical, transformational insight which revealed a profound new depth and power to the teachings of the Bible. In the tradition of Christian Mystics such as Meister Eckhart, St John of the Cross and Father Bede Griffiths, this miraculous insight reveals that oneness with God is, in reality, our original, natural state. Non-duality opens a new understanding of formally enigmatic scriptures where the reader is led, step by step, to their own personal experience of rest and liberation in oneness with God.

Made in the USA
Charleston, SC
12 October 2015